THE PRACTICAL STRATEGIES SERIES
IN GIFTED EDUCATION

series editors
FRANCES A. KARNES & KRISTEN R. STEPHENS

When Gifted Students Underachieve: What You Can Do About It

Sylvia Rimm

Routledge
Taylor & Francis Group

NEW YORK AND LONDON

First published 2006 by Prufrock Press, Inc.

Published in 2021 by Routledge
605 Third Avenue, New York, NY 10017
2 Park Square, Milton Park, Abingdon, Oxon OX14 4RN

Routledge is an imprint of the Taylor & Francis Group, an informa business

ISBN 13: 978-1-59363-193-2 (pbk)
ISBN 13: 978-1-00-323955-0 (ebk)

Contents

The Practical Strategies Series in Gifted Education offers teachers, counselors, administrators, parents, and other interested parties up-to-date instructional techniques and information on a variety of issues pertinent to the field of gifted education. Each guide addresses a focused topic and is written by scholars with authority on the issue. Several guides have been published. Among the titles are:

- *Acceleration Strategies for Teaching Gifted Learners*
- *Curriculum Compacting: An Easy Start to Differentiating for High-Potential Students*
- *Enrichment Opportunities for Gifted Learners*
- *Independent Study for Gifted Learners*
- *Motivating Gifted Students*
- *Questioning Strategies for Teaching the Gifted*
- *Social & Emotional Teaching Strategies*
- *Using Media & Technology With Gifted Learners*

For a current listing of available guides within the series, please contact Prufrock Press at (800) 998-2208 or visit http://www.prufrock.com.

Underachievement by gifted students has long puzzled educators, parents, and even gifted students themselves. Although definitions of underachievement vary, all include a discrepancy between some measure of a child's ability and his or her achievement (Baum, Renzulli, & Hébert, 1995; Butler-Por, 1987; Colangelo, Kerr, Christensen, & Maxey, 1993; Dowdall & Colangelo, 1982; Emerick, 1992; Lupart & Pyryt, 1996; Redding, 1990; Rimm, 1997; Supplee, 1990; Whitmore, 1980; Wolfle, 1991).

The variations in definitions of underachievement come from how ability and achievement are measured. Thus, some definitions rely specifically on differences between IQ and achievement test scores, while others might use grades or school production as measures of achievement. These operational definitions can cause great differences in how and why many gifted students are considered to be underachievers. For example, students who show no discrepancy between IQ and achievement test scores might not be recognized as underachievers by some definitions, but would, nevertheless, be considered underachievers by their teachers and parents if they earn poor grades in school. Additionally, using precise test scores alone would give one an underestimate of the number of underachievers. Reis and McCoach (2000) indicate that although precise operational definitions provide clarity for research, they lack flexibility for identifying specific causes of underachievement.

There's rarely a clear cause and effect relationship when a child underachieves. Instead, there are usually multiple and complex causes of underachievement. Reis and McCoach (2002) developed two categories of causes: environmental factors and factors within the individual. Within the environmental category, unchallenging classrooms, peer pressures, isolation from classmates, and family dynamics are included. The individual category consists of internalizing issues, such as depression and anxiety, and externalizing issues including rebellion and nonconformity, learning problems, deficits in self-regulation, and social immaturity.

Cultural diversity represents a further variation in the environmental factors that cause underachievement. There is little research on the unique barriers faced by minority students who underachieve (Ford, 1996; Reis, Hébert, Diaz, Maxfield, & Ratley, 1995). Ford and Tyson (2004) maintain that some educators operate in a culturally blind fashion and pretend cultural differences don't exist. Furthermore, if current identification approaches are biased, as many assume, and fail to identify gifted minority students (Baldwin, 1987; Ford; Frasier & Passow, 1994), they will also fail to identify underachieving gifted students from these populations. Also, family and peer definitions of achievement often differ in varying subcultures, sometimes making it difficult to use interventions successful in the mainstream culture.

Characteristics of Underachievement

Underachievers tend to be disorganized. They often dawdle, forget homework, lose assignments, and misplace books; they daydream, don't listen, look out the window, or talk too much to other children. They have poor study skills or none at all. Some underachievers are slow and perfectionistic and don't finish their work. On the other hand, some will complete their assignments quickly, but are too concerned about being finished first to do quality work.

Some underachievers never read books for fun, while others immerse themselves in reading as an escape. Such students especially like to read when they're supposed to be doing homework. Television, computers, or video games may also serve as alternative escapes for underachieving students.

Creative underachievers may have many unusual ideas, but rarely bring their ideas to closure. They seem unable to complete what they begin. Their parents often refer to them as "marching to the beat of a different drummer," and they may be described as "too creative" for school (Smutny, 2004).

Underachievers often use innumerable defenses. School is "boring" when they're young and "irrelevant" when they're older. Their poor grades, which they say don't matter, are typically blamed on "terrible teachers." They think drama, sports, music, or having a social life is more important than schoolwork. "Who wants to be a geek anyway?" they retort. Some call achievement their parents' goal, not theirs, and blame their problems on "unfair" comparisons with siblings or "unfair" pressures by their parents. All underachievers are definitely not the same, and most can exhibit any number of these characteristics.

Internal Locus of Control

Underlying the poor study habits, disorganization, and excuses about their underachievement is a feeling of lack of personal control over their educational success. Underachievers don't really believe they can reach their goals, even if they work harder. Siegle (2004) describes such feelings as a lack of self-efficacy, and he indicates that people with low self-efficacy are more likely to avoid challenging activities. They set their goals either too high or too low; as a result, they guarantee failure. Such students often want to be millionaires, professional football or baseball players, rock stars, computer geniuses, Olympic gymnasts, or company presidents, and they have magical ideas about the efforts necessary to arrive at these lofty goals. They haven't yet discovered what *work* actually means and can't build firm self-confidence because they haven't learned a real sense of effort.

It's from actual achievement that one develops confidence. Underachievers have denied themselves the opportunity to build confidence because they direct their energies toward avoiding the relationship between effort and outcome. Siegle (2004) adds that, "years of failure can lower students' confidence . . . so they refuse to risk another failure. . . . " (p. 31). Figure 1, Rimm's laws, addresses the development of self-confidence, as well as many other issues relating to children affected by underachievement discussed throughout this book.

Competition

We live in a competitive society, and even families and schools are competitive with one another. Underachievers often

1. Children are more likely to be achievers if their parents join together to give the same clear and positive message about school effort and expectations.
2. Children can learn appropriate behaviors more easily if they have effective models to imitate.
3. Communication about a child between adults (referential speaking) within the child's hearing dramatically affects children's behaviors and self-perception.
4. Overreaction by parents to children's successes and failures leads them to feel either intense pressure to succeed, or despair and discouragement in dealing with failure.
5. Children feel more tension when they are worrying about their work than when they are doing that work.
6. Children develop self-confidence through struggle.
7. Deprivation and excess frequently exhibit the same symptoms.
8. Children develop confidence and an internal sense of control if power is given to them in gradually increasing increments as they show maturity and responsibility.
9. Children become oppositional if one adult allies with them against a parent or a teacher, making them more powerful than an adult.
10. Adults should avoid confrontations with children unless they are sure they can control the outcomes.
11. Children will become achievers only if they learn to function in competition.
12. Children will continue to achieve if they usually see the relationship between the learning process and its outcomes.

Figure 1. Rimm's laws

Note. From *Why Bright Kids Get Poor Grades—And What You Can Do About It* by S. B. Rimm, 1995, p. xviii. Copyright ©1995 by S. B. Rimm. Reprinted with permission.

have highly competitive feelings, but they may not be obvious. They aspire to be winners, and yet, they are poor losers. If they don't believe they can win, they may quit before they begin, or they may select only school experiences in which they're certain of victory. They're competitive, internally pressured children who've not learned to cope with defeat, and they lack resilience. As Rimm's law #11 asserts, "Children will become achievers only if they learn to function in competition."

It's not possible to be productive in our society or in our schools until one learns to cope with competition. Coping with competition requires understanding that winning and losing are always temporary occurrences. Children who learn to lose without being devastated and use failure experiences to grow will begin to achieve in the classroom and in society.

Learning to compete effectively is central to achievement in school. Underachievers often manipulate their families and school environments in their fear of failure. They learn to avoid competition unless they can win, and in the process, they miss learning important skills. As their underachievement cycle continues, they begin to feel less and less capable. Their fear of failure increases, and their sense of efficacy decreases. There seems to be little written in the underachievement research literature about the place of competition, yet in this author's research on identification of underachievement, factor analyses of items for the Achievement Identification Measure (AIM) yielded results related to competition (Rimm, 1986).

Valuing the Task

The Siegle and McCoach model of underachievement (Siegle et al., 2002) maintains that valuing school tasks is a foundational underlying cause of underachievement. While this group has found that pointing out the value of the school task increases motivation to achieve and is, thus, a powerful tool for reversal of underachievement, clinical findings suggest children who lack self-efficacy or feel inadequate in competitive settings frequently may use claims that schoolwork is useless as a defense mechanism (Rimm, 1995). While pointing out the relevance of the task enhances motivation temporarily for some, other underachieving students refuse to be convinced that learning English grammar or reading Shakespeare are relevant, because they find the tasks uninteresting, difficult, or threatening. Thus pointing out the relevance of the task is appropriate, but works best with children who are not using "irrelevance" as a defense mechanism.

Parents have been blamed too frequently and too easily for the pressures felt by gifted children, but usually the pressures are more complicated than they appear. There are four common pressure areas gifted underachievers frequently experience.

Pressure to Be the Smartest

The intense feeling that one must be the smartest all the time shows itself in many ways. It's manifested in the children whose waving, enthusiastic hands indicate they will willingly monopolize class discussion with their displays of brilliance, or the children who put others down as dumb or stupid in order to feel smart. It's shown in the youth who rush through their work because "smart" has come to mean "quick and easy" to them, and the ones who can't get started on an assigned essay because they can't decide on the perfect writing topic. Such pressure is displayed in the children who change the subject to discuss a different issue when they can't answer a question. Students who feel pressured to be *the* smartest argue endlessly with parents and teachers and appear to be completely blind to anyone else's point of view, because it's more important to prove they're smart and right than to consider another's ideas or feelings. For these children, their identity is so tied to their intellectual giftedness they fear that mistakes or gaps in their knowledge will unmask inadequacies.

Children with unusual learning styles, or learning styles that don't fit with typical instructional methods in the classroom, are particularly susceptible to this pressure, and although they may recognize their own giftedness, these children may avoid school assignments when they're not as productive as they wish to be. Learning disabilities related to handwriting, math, or reading also feel threatening to gifted children, who then fear they are not as smart as test scores document (Baum, 2004).

Pressure to Be Different

Some children feel pressured to be different from their peers and even their family members. Every reader has experienced that sense of wanting to complete a project or activity in a unique or unusual way. In some children, that sense becomes the pressure to be unique or to do something that's highly creative. If you multiply those feelings of pressure to be different by a thousand, you might have a sense of what some children feel when they get dressed in the morning, when they write a story or composition, when they speak up in a class discussion, or when they face an independent project in school. Here are some statements by children that reveal the extreme pressure they feel to be creative:

- "I would like math if I could have 6 apples and 8 apples equal something different every time. I hate to always write the same answer."
- "I can't possibly hand my reports in on time. It always takes me longer to make them as unique as I want them to be."
- "Have you ever met anyone as different as I am? You should see my room!"

Being creative for these children means being the *most* different.

Pressure to Be Popular

Parents and teachers of elementary school children often emphasize good social adjustment. Gifted children often do adjust well in elementary school and don't appear pressured. They learn to enjoy the comforts of social acceptance, although some may play down their intelligence, even minimizing their use of extensive vocabulary, lest they offend peers.

This "good adjustment" during elementary school brings forth a different pressure during preadolescence. By then, social adjustment translates to popularity, and this forces children into value systems that may differ significantly from what their parents and teachers earlier described as social adjustment (Rimm, 2005). Depending on the peer environment, the popular message may involve positive activities, or it may mean alcohol, drugs, and sexual promiscuity. Popularity also may mean *not* getting A's and *not* working too hard in school.

Pressure to Be Loyal

Racial allegiance issues may cause considerable pressure on gifted minorities to underachieve (Ford, Grantham, & Milner, 2004). Some gifted children come from homes and neighborhoods that may not value academic achievement. Their parents may have had unfortunate school experiences and still hold resentment toward the educational system. Their family and friends may be untrusting of teachers, and may only send their children to school because it's required. Gifted children from such environments who are academically successful may be taunted at home as being "uppity" or, in the case of some ethnic minorities, "acting White." They may feel pressured to hide their accomplishments from parents and peers, or chastised for doing homework or reading too much. They may feel torn between school messages to learn and achieve, and cultural and environmental messages that consider learning to be boring and a waste of time.

Where do Pressures Originate?

Children's feelings of pressure can come from their own excellent performance, as well as from the praise or pleasure from parents, teachers, or peers their intelligence, creativity, or adjustment attracts. Whether adults compare their performance to others or whether children do it on their own, viewing themselves as the smartest, most creative, or most popular among friends encourages students to continue to want the feelings of exhilaration that accompany being *the* best. For young gifted children, attracting attention using their extensive vocabulary, their clever and original ideas, or their sunny disposition and beauty seems relatively easy. Learning to share the attention that excellence attracts becomes more difficult as they mature, because they compare themselves to other capable children who may attract similar attention. Furthermore, academic excellence, creative production, popularity, and cultural expectations often cause conflicting pressures by the time students reach middle school (Rimm, 2005). At this stage, students can easily give up on one area of interest to favor another that seems more appealing, such as giving up on academic excellence in hopes of excelling in popularity, expressing their creativity through outlandish dress, or experimenting with drugs.

Motivation and Pressure

It isn't easy to prevent gifted children from experiencing pressure, because motivation and pressure are so closely tied together. Stress occurs when children have high expectations for themselves, but haven't learned to manage the path to achieving those expectations. Motivation may involve the same high expectations for excellence, but then children have learned that hard work or effort can lead them to accomplish those expectations. Although they, too, may dream of impossibly high accomplishments, students who are motivated rather than pressured set benchmarks to achieve along the way. For example, motivated children who dream of becoming great scientists willingly study for science exams to earn the A's that will permit them to get into a good college program; whereas when pressured, gifted children might dream of making a scientific breakthrough while procrastinating and playing computer games instead of studying, hoping they are smart enough to pull an A on the test by merely having listened to the teacher in class. Even if they only achieve a B, they can brag about getting a B without studying, and that might make them feel smarter than others who had to study hard to earn their A's.

Preventing and Reversing Pressures That Lead to Underachievement

Keeping children motivated instead of pressured is a challenge to parents and educators. Using praise words like *smart* instead of *smartest* or *brilliant* could prevent some of the pressure placed on children, and praise for the process of achievement or effort usually encourages children to be motivated (Dweck, 2000). Calling them *hard workers* and *good thinkers*, noticing their perseverance and their love of challenge, and telling children that the smarter they are, the harder they'll work and inversely, the harder they work, the smarter they'll be, can give them some feelings of control over their achievement. You may actually increase their courage by explaining to them that self-confidence grows only if they take on risks and challenges.

Instead of reassuring underachievers of their brilliance or creativity, it's better to admire their hard work ethic (Dweck, 2000). That may not be as exciting to them, but at least it will relieve some of the pressure. They might as well learn early that there's no permanent first place. No matter how smart or creative they are, there are always others who are smarter or more creative. Learning to feel good about doing *their* best, rather than doing only *the* best, can be motivating.

Protecting Their Fragile Self-Concepts

Underachievers' avoidance patterns are typically psycho-logical defense mechanisms. They perpetuate defense mechanisms to protect their fragile self-concepts when they aren't certain they can perform to the expectations initially set by parents and teachers. Underachievers typically equate giftedness with the ability to learn quickly and easily. Thus, challenging work may appear threatening to them. They worry it could reveal that they're not as gifted as expected. The avoidance of tasks and the excuses they give protect them temporarily, but steal their opportunities for developing self-discipline, educational skills, interests and most importantly, efficacy or genuine intellectual self-confidence. Underachievers generally defend their fragile self-concepts in two different directions—by dependence or dominance, or for some, a combination of both. These dependent and dominant defense mechanisms eventually begin to feel natural to children, yet parents and teachers still feel frustrated by these mechanisms, because they can't seem to encourage their children's steady achievement.

Dependence and Dominance

The dependence pattern is often masked by insecurity, immaturity, passivity, or learning disabilities. Dependent underachievers ask for more help than they require. They tend not to take initiative, and may insist on having parents sit with them while they do their homework. They complain, whine, and are continuously negative, or they request help more frequently than necessary. Dominant underachievers are more vociferous in arguing about why they shouldn't have to do their work—they tend to blame teachers or parents for their problems. They like to pick and choose only the schoolwork they enjoy, and often claim that routine work is inappropriate for their giftedness. They're creative to the point of opposition and insist on wielding power without respect for the rights of others.

Delisle and Galbraith (2002) view somewhat similar patterns but have named the dependent underachievers *underachievers*, and the dominant underachievers *selective consumers*. For example, their *underachievers* tend to withdraw when faced with challenge, while their *selective consumers* are more likely to rebel (Delisle, 2004). Reis and McCoach (2002) referred to a similar dependence/dominance pattern as *internalizing* and *externalizing* underachievement.

Young children and even some adolescents aren't likely to understand why they lack achievement motivation; it will take the leadership and insight of parents and teachers to guide them toward achievement. Adults often parent and teach intuitively. Intuition, or good common sense, works well with children who are engaged in academic learning and achievement. For children exhibiting dependent and dominant avoidance patterns, counterintuitive responses to parenting and teaching are often more effective than intuitive responses, in that the intuitive responses have already reinforced the underachievement and have been proven ineffective. For example, dependent underachievers frequently ask for more help than they need. Intuitively, parents and educators respond with help and reassurances that have been asked for, when instead these children need encouragement to persevere and continue independently so they can build confidence. On the other hand, dominant children push limits, make excuses, and blame others for unfinished work. Again, adults tend to get angry, threaten punishments, or overpunish children, accelerating the battle between adult and student.

Counterintuitively, hearing out the child forms an alliance and helps the child sense that the adult is supportive of him or her, thus compromise is possible and consequences can be firmly set, but by reasonable agreement. Underachievement can be reversed, and dependence or extreme dominance can be modified to help children live more satisfying and productive lives. Once children become productive, they're more willing to admit that they like their achieving lifestyle better than their former patterns of avoidance. Furthermore, relationships with parents, teachers, siblings, and peers improve with their new productivity and confidence.

Classroom environments also make a difference in the behavior of underachieving students (Rimm, 1995). As noted earlier, an underlying characteristic revealed in most studies of underachievement is a lack of personal locus of control. That is, underachievers don't internalize the relationship between effort and outcome. They'll say, "The teacher gave me that grade," "I got lucky," or "I must be dumb," rather than "I studied hard and earned that grade," or "The test was harder than I expected, so I'll prepare better next time."

Illustrated in Figure 2 are the potential classroom relationships between efforts and outcomes. The figure shows how the appropriate relationship will support children's achievement motivation. Quadrant 1 illustrates the appropriate relationship that fosters an achievement orientation. Quadrants 2, 3, and 4 show unbalanced relationships, which destroy the relationship between efforts and outcomes and initiate defensive and avoidance patterns, which in turn foster underachievement.

Children in Quadrant 1 feel bright, creative, and approved of by parents and teachers. They're usually motivated to earn good grades and approval from adults and friends; hopefully, they also feel a sense of intrinsic and extrinsic satisfaction from

+ OUTCOMES –

	+	–
+	Quadrant 1 + + Achievers	Quadrant 2 + – Underachievers
–	Quadrant 3 – + Underachievers	Quadrant 4 – – Underachievers

EFFORT

Figure 2. Relationship between effort and outcomes

Note. From *Guidebook—Underachievement Syndrome: Causes and Cures,* by S. B. Rimm, M. Cornale, R. Manos, and J. Behrend, 1989, p. 289. Copyright ©1989 by Apple Publishing. Reprinted with permission of the author.

their accomplishments. They set realistically high goals, work hard, and understand perseverance. When they occasionally slip, their grades go down, thus reinforcing the connection of hard work to success. Their resumed effort brings success again. As Rimm's law #12 maintains, "Children will continue to achieve if they usually see the relationship between the learning process and its outcomes."

Quadrant 2 represents a transition to underachievement where efforts begin appropriately, but goals are set too high. The "too-high" goals or outcomes may come in a highly competitive school environment where, despite a child's intelligence and good study skills, good grades don't feel attainable. If parents set expectations beyond children's abilities, and of course some do, these expectations will have the same impact as that of goals set too high—eventual underachievement. Children who have learning disabilities or unusual learning styles may experience Quadrant 2, because even if they work hard, achieving their goals may seem impossible. Schultz (2000) points out that twice-exceptional children (those with giftedness and learning disabilities) may mask either their giftedness, their disability, or both. They may be "held captive within the prisons of remediation" (Baum, 2004, p.13). Quadrant 2's unrealistic goals can make children feel "dumb," even if they are highly intelligent.

Quadrant 3 illustrates the most typical dilemma for gifted children. They begin by feeling positive about school, but they're not sufficiently challenged. They learn that achievement is easy, and learning and studying are effortless. As long as their grades continue to be high, they exhibit no problem behaviors. When the curriculum becomes more challenging, some students learn more appropriate study habits. Others hide from the perceived threat such challenge brings. They invent or discover rituals that prevent them from making further effort. Many underachieving gifted students have said, "If you're smart, schoolwork should be easy."

Gifted programming that challenges students can help prevent Quadrant 3 underachievement. Accelerated and enriched curriculum that stimulates gifted students and allows them to enjoy challenges can help them recognize that giftedness prospers when they work hard. Homogeneous grouping, creative thinking programs, and subject and grade acceleration provide opportunities for gifted children to become accustomed to challenging work. Furthermore, if the curriculum is intrinsically interesting and feels relevant to their lives, children will more likely be motivated to put forth effort, and are less likely to feel threatened. There are some excellent books on differentiating curriculum, which can help teachers provide classroom environments that increase gifted children's sense of efficacy (Karnes & Bean 2005; Smutny & von Fremd, 2004; Tomlinson, 2004; Tomlinson et al., 2002; VanTassel-Baska & Little, 2003; Winebrenner, 2001).

Quadrant 4 represents an advanced stage of underachievement. It results after children described in Quadrant 2 or 3 have functioned as underachievers for a period of time. Quadrant 4 underachievement takes place when children's efforts and skills have had deficiencies for so long that they've given up on reasonable goal setting. Teachers and parents often doubt these children's abilities. Parents may recall that their children were smart at some point in the past, but they may be willing to settle for them earning barely passing grades.

Quadrant 4 underachievement can be difficult to reverse, and sometimes requires therapeutic help. Parents and teachers may be able to prevent Quadrant 4 problems by correcting problems in Quadrant 2 or 3. Identifying learning disabilities, learning style differences, and providing appropriately challenging curriculum are important steps in both preventing and reversing underachievement. The mismatch between children's abilities and curriculum, which is often a root of underachievement, must be corrected for children to become motivated (Reis, 1998; Reis et al., 1995; Whitmore, 1986).

Family values about school achievement do matter to children. If parents value achievement, children are more likely to achieve in school (Baker, Bridger, & Evans, 1998; Brown, Mounts, Lamborn, & Steinberg, 1993; Rimm & Lowe, 1988). If one or both parents have had negative experiences in school, they may convey those feelings to their children and may unintentionally encourage negative feelings in them. If they recall school as having been boring, and remind their children of their boredom, children may indeed avoid getting interested or involved in schoolwork. Some parents even accept their children's underachievement because they themselves had been underachievers. They assume their children have inherited the problem and feel helpless about doing anything to solve it. Parents who are disinterested in education also may foster underachievement (Jeon & Feldhusen, 1993).

Family Trauma

Even when families have healthy attitudes about achievement, temporary trauma can distract students from achievement (Battle, 2002). Death, divorce, or physical or emotional illness in the family may claim a student's attention and cause school success to seem irrelevant.

Parenting Styles

Taylor (1994) found that parents of high achieving students tended to favor an authoritative parenting style, and multiple studies have found that families that are either too restrictive or too lenient foster underachievement (Clark, 2002; Pendarvis, Howley, & Howley, 1990; Weiner, 1992). Rimm and Lowe (1988) found that conflicts between parents related to their child's achievement efforts and goals also make a great difference. In 95% of the underachieving gifted student's families studied, one parent played the role of the parent that challenged and disciplined the child, and the other took on the role of the parent that protected the child. Consistency between parents (a united front) seems even more important than specific parenting style.

It seems crucial that the adults who guide children's lives do so in a united and reasonably consistent way (Rimm & Lowe, 1988). Even though adults may have some differences in their preferred styles of parenting, children should perceive fairly similar expectations, efforts, and limits from both parents. Compromises and mutual respect between parents and other family members can help encourage children's motivation for success and respect for other adults. If children face parents who have contradictory expectations and lack the confidence to meet the expectations of one of their parents, they often turn to the other parent who usually not only unconditionally supports them, but also unconsciously teaches them "the easy way out." The kind and caring parents, without recognizing the problem they're causing their children, unintentionally overprotect them when they face challenges. When children have grown up in an environment where one adult has provided an easy way out for them, they develop the habit of avoiding challenges.

Two of Rimm's laws summarize this important issue: law #1—"Children are more likely to be achievers if their parents join together to give the same clear and positive message about school effort and expectation," and law #9—"Children become oppositional if one adult allies with them against a parent or a teacher, making them more powerful than an adult."

Children in today's society may have multiple parents and caregivers. Sometimes they have one parent and sometimes they have four. Sometimes grandparents, aunts, uncles, or nannies assist in parenting. According to a Census Bureau report, only half of this country's children live in traditional two-parent families (Usdansky, 1994). The team balancing act increases in complexity when there are three or four parents involved. Each parent is desperately anxious to provide the best parenting in order to keep their child's love. After divorce, parents may believe they can tempt children to love them by protecting them the most or doing too much for them.

There are four competitive and destructive rituals that take place between parents. And, there are variations of these rituals that involve stepparents, grandparents, aunts, and uncles. If adults sabotage each other in their efforts to help children, it almost always results in underachievement. The good news is that since this sabotage is usually unintentional, it can be changed. When parents manage to join together and support each other, it encourages children to move forward. Furthermore, when children do move forward, the conflict between parents often decreases. Reis and McCoach (2000) observed that it is often difficult to determine if the family discord fosters the underachievement, or the underachievement increases family discord.

The Parent-Teacher United Front

Respect for teachers improves students' motivation (Rimm, 1995). Parent-teacher conflicts emerge mainly because some teachers have different philosophies than some parents about how their gifted children should be taught. Parents may believe their philosophies are better than those held by their children's teachers and vice versa. When teachers and parents disagree on how children should be taught, it can destroy the united parent–teacher front. If the philosophy of the parents differs from that of the teacher so that it provides an easy way out for children or if a parent describes the teacher's philosophy as inappropriate, irrelevant, or boring, another excuse is created for children not to accomplish what the teacher expects. Consider that children are sitting in a class-room and are faced with tasks or assignments, with some that are interesting, and some not so interesting. If they've received the message from their parents that these aren't worthwhile projects, why would these children consider it important to fulfill the teacher's expectations? They know they can come home and find an empathetic ear in their mother or father who will basically agree that the assignment was inappropriate to their interest or intelligence.

If parents want their children to achieve in school, they should give clear directions to their children about respecting teachers, by letting them know that teachers are people who are devoted to making a difference for society through education. If respect is shown to educators, it will go a long way toward encouraging children to feel positive about their teachers and about school. Parents of gifted children do need to be advocates for their children's education, but they need to advocate in respectful voices.

The Rimm (1995) Trifocal Model provides an easy-to-apply framework for intervention in schools and clinics. It includes six steps of which the first five may apply to all under-achievers. In step six, parents and teachers can select those modifications that are most appropriate to their underachieving student or child. In the clinical setting, the average reversal time for underachievement using this model is 6 months. The time varies with the intensity of the problem, the age of the child, and most importantly, with the consistency and perseverance of parents and teachers. Very young children take only a few months, while high school students usually require at least a full school year. They're often difficult to turn around because of peer pressures and the risks of alcohol, drugs, and other temptations. Figure 3 illustrates the Trifocal Model.

Step 1—Assessment

The main purpose of this first step is to determine the extent and direction of a child's underachievement. There are both formal and informal methods of assessment. The formal approaches include group or individual intelligence tests,

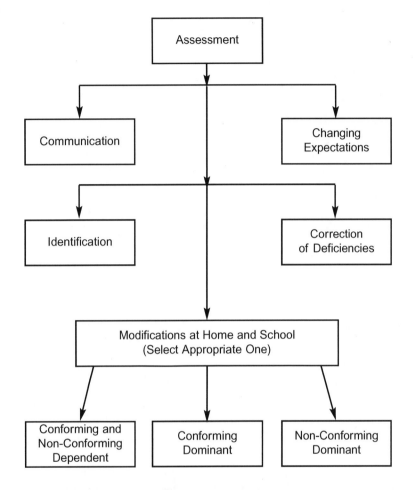

Figure 3. TRIFOCAL Model for reversing underachievement

Note. From *Why Bright Kids Get Poor Grades—And What You Can Do About It,* by S. B. Rimm, 1995, p. 162. Copyright ©1995 by S. B. Rimm. Reprinted with permission.

achievement tests, creativity tests, and underachievement inventories, all of which can be administered by a school or clinical psychologist. Informal evaluations involve the questioning and observation of children by their parents and teachers.

Formal Assessment

Although IQ tests are referred to as "intelligence" tests, educators now realize they measure only some kinds of intelligence. In addition, cultural environments and learning, as well as the individual's inherent intelligence, affect scores on IQ tests.

Despite the many limitations of IQ tests, they're still helpful (when used cautiously) to predict how well children will perform in various educational environments. The results also help identify strengths and weaknesses in children's learning styles, and, in some cases, even learning disabilities. While full-scale IQ scores may indicate giftedness, individual subtest scores of individually administered tests can show developmental delays, specific disabilities, or skill deficits. It may be assumed that children are capable in all areas, when in fact, some types of learning are truly difficult.

Although research has shown that average IQs tend to stay fairly constant throughout people's lives, clinical experiences with elementary and secondary underachievers indicate otherwise. Children who underachieve in school for many years often show large declines in IQ scores (Rimm, Cornale, Manos, & Behrend, 1989). New testing can result in scores 10–20 points lower than earlier tests. Yet, for children who reverse their underachievement, both IQ and achievement test scores often increase.

Other formal assessments that provide help in identifying and describing both the extent and direction of underachievement include parent inventories, teacher observation scales, and child self-report inventories, which can be completed at home or in the classroom. Achievement Identification Measure (AIM; Rimm, 1986), Group Achievement Identification Measure (GAIM; Rimm, 1987), and Achievement Identification Measure-Teacher Observation (AIM-TO; Rimm, 1988) were developed specifically for assessing underachievement. A description of dimension scores of AIM is included in Figure 4. They are helpful in quantifying underachievement problems and enhancing communication between parents and teachers.

Dimension	Explanation
Competition	High scorers enjoy competition whether they win or lose. They are good sports and handle victories graciously. They don't give up easily. Low scorers get depressed, cry, complain, or lose their temper when they do poorly at something. They tend to brag as winners. They are not skillful in peer relationships because they want to be in charge or prefer not to play.
Responsibility	High scorers are independent and responsible in their schoolwork. They tend to be well organized and bring activities to closure. Low scorers depend on adults for help and attention and do not plan or organize their school responsibilities. They may also misbehave in attention-getting ways.
Control	High scorers are comfortable in school or home settings without dominating or manipulating parents, teachers, or peers. Low scorers tend to be dominant or controlling children who have typically been given too much power as preschoolers by one or both parents. They expect to be the center of attention and to be in control of their peers, their classroom, and their family, and feel angry and out of control even when they are subjected to reasonable discipline.
Achievement communication	Children who score high are receiving clear and consistent messages from parents about the importance of learning and good grades. Their parents have communicated positive feelings about their own school experiences and there is consistency in messages between mother and father. Low scorers have parents who give contradictory or negative messages about achievement in what they do and/or in what they say.
Respect	High scorers are respectful toward their parents and other adults. Low scorers are rebellious or disobedient and ignore their parents' requests and requirements. There is frequently inconsistency in the discipline philosophy of the parents.

Figure 4. Dimensions for
Achievement Identification Measure (AIM)

Note. From *Achievement Identification Measure* by Sylvia B. Rimm, 1986, pp. 2-4. Copyright ©1986 by Educational Assessment Service. Reprinted with permission.

Informal Assessment

The informal approaches to assessing underachievement in children may be apparent. If teachers have told parents for years that their children aren't working up to their abilities, parents can safely assume that the problem is real.

The descriptions of underachievers discussed earlier may help identify patterns of underachievement. Dependent children unconsciously manipulate people in their environments covertly in ways that require more than the typical assistance and encouragement. Their words and body language reach out for more help than they should need. Dependent underachievers are often mistaken as having learning disabilities, and learning disabled gifted children can easily be mistaken as underachievers.

Dominant children relate to adults in their environments in more overtly aggressive ways. Because they function comfortably only when they're dominating a situation, they feel out of control when they're not mastering their environment. They'll argue and debate. They'll trap adults into irrationality, and then use that adult's behaviors as an excuse for not complying. Furthermore, they'll complain about and often successfully persuade other adults to side with them against the first adult.

Children who mainly exhibit the "poor me" characteristics can be classified as dependent, while those who continuously challenge others are usually dominant. However, keep in mind that these categories and prototypes aren't always distinct, but may blend in any one child. By adolescence, most young people exhibit both dependent and dominant characteristics.

Identifying the child's main symptoms will help determine the best ways to modify parents' and teachers' approaches that reinforce underachieving behaviors. When observing children at home and in school, it's most important to note how and for what behaviors they gain adult and peer attention. Knowledge of the ways they attract adults to them will help discriminate between dependent and dominant underachievers. The usual pace of dependent children is slow and cautious, while dominant children are more likely to be fast and impulsive. Every child is unique, and these labels are used only to focus on main characteristics.

Figure 5 summarizes the dependent and dominant manipulations. It's important to remember that determining if these are real needs or only manipulations will depend on the frequency of use and whether they protect the child from risk and responsibility. All normal children exhibit these behaviors occasionally, but underachievers frequently use these manipulations as defense mechanisms so they don't have to cope with the risk of finding out they're not *the* best at a certain task. The manipulations are usually not conscious, mean, or deliberate. They are, however, habitual and dysfunctional, and will reinforce underachievement patterns.

Step 2—Communication

Underachievement can be reversed most effectively when parents, teachers, and students work together. Although it's possible for teachers to help students without parent cooperation, it's much easier to work closely with parents, and the reversal process will take place more quickly.

Figure 6 outlines suggested topics to discuss with parents. Teachers should observe students to notice as many strong areas as possible. Their description of strengths will assure parents they care about their child. Weaknesses and problems, on the other hand, don't all need to be described in the first conference, lest parents become discouraged and view their children's problems as impossible to correct. Teachers should explain class performance in straightforward language, avoiding educational jargon. A description of both the grade level they're working at and what can be expected of their gifted children will be helpful. Discussing dependence and dominance with parents may reveal that children follow similar patterns at both home and school or, indeed, that children may battle parents at home (dominance) while asking for too much help at school (dependence). Planning study time at home will reveal whether parents are capable of following through and supervising homework appropriately. For parents who can't take charge for any num-

Dependent	Dominant
Help me.	Admire me, praise me, applaud me.
Nag me.	Do not criticize me.
Protect me.	Disagree with me.
Feel sorry for me.	Give me.
Love me.	Be mine.
Shelter me.	See my difference.
	How far can I push?

Figure 5. Dependent and dominant manipulation

Note. From *Why Bright Kids Get Poor Grades—And What You Can Do About It,* by S. B. Rimm, 1995, p. 201. Copyright ©1995 by S. B. Rimm. Reprinted with permission of the author.

ber of reasons, after-school or in-school study plans may have to be devised.

Accountability communication between teachers and parents is important because underachievers almost always lie about their schoolwork. Teachers may want to state that gently to parents. Underachievers may bend the truth, report A's, but not D's and F's, claim they have no homework when they prefer not to do it, excuse themselves from efforts by saying they don't recall the assignments, and blame teachers for losing assignments they haven't accomplished or handed in.

Research finds home-to-school notes are important, and consistent use of such notes is essential in establishing a communication system among parents, students, and teachers regarding student progress (Nahmias, 1995). Home-to-school notes promote consistency in expectations and help teachers and parents develop a common language. These notes may be simple check sheets or lists for reporting student behavior and/or academic work. Using daily or weekly journals is help-

1. Strengths and abilities
2. Weaknesses and problems
3. Grade level of class performance
4. Peer relationships
5. Dependence or dominance
6. Homework and study plan
7. Accountability communication
8. Contracting suggestions
9. Exchange of readings and/or tapes

Figure 6. Parent-teacher conference topics

Note. From *Why Bright Kids Get Poor Grades: The Gifted Underachiever and How You Can Help,* day-long teacher workshop, conducted by S. B. Rimm for Catawba County Schools, Hickory, NC, 2004b. Copyright ©2004 by S. B. Rimm. Reprinted with permission.

ful when more elaborate information is needed (Williams & Cartledge, 1997). Teachers and parents also have opportunities to regularly communicate through formal and informal meetings and telephone calls. The key is to promote good communication so that the parent, teacher, and student can become a collaborative team (Bos, Nahmias, & Urban, 1999).

Figure 7 provides a sample form that teachers might send home weekly. Similar forms or notes can be used daily for elementary school children. Signed assignment notebooks or e-mails are also ideal for keeping parents abreast of their children's efforts.

Notes or forms can be shared and discussed by children and their parents at daily or weekly achievement-monitoring conferences. If parents are actively involved, children receive assessments of their progress twice—once from their teachers who distribute the message, and again from their parents. If teachers are undertaking the underachievement reversal process without parent participation, a key teacher or counselor could be the regular recipient of communications about progress. The person with whom the student reviews his progress can be called a *child advocate.*

Parents or advocates can plan achievement meetings with children on either a daily or weekly basis. For children in primary grades, a brief daily review of accomplishments and rein-

Student   Teacher
name_____   name_____   Date_____

Subject: _____

Approximate grade for week: _____ (optional)

Assignments completed:

_____All   _____Most   _____Half   _____Less than half

Classroom effort:

_____Excellent _____Satisfactory _____Fair   _____Unsatisfactory

Behavior:

_____Excellent _____Satisfactory _____Fair   _____Unsatisfactory

Comments and missing assignments:

_____

_____

_____

_____

Thank you very much for your help.

Figure 7. Weekly evaluation form

Note. From *Why Bright Kids Get Poor Grades—And What You Can Do About It,* by S. B. Rimm, 1995, p. 211. Copyright ©1995 by S. B. Rimm. Reprinted with permission.

forcements is appropriate. As a child's achievement and behavior improve, parent and advocate meetings should be set for a regular weekly time. Secondary students should have weekly meetings initially. When they show fairly consistent effort, meetings can move to biweekly or monthly intervals.

It's important to keep the tone of advocate or parent sessions with students positive and instructive. These sessions should provide children with the opportunity to review their gains, receive encouragement, and deal with both the positive and negative consequences of their new efforts. They become the means for assessing and reinforcing efforts, setting goals, and clarifying consequences. Whether or not rewards are used to encourage achievement, progress reports from a teacher are an important element in developing children's efficacy. The communications build a connection between effort and outcomes.

Many schools prefer to have children circulate a form from teacher to teacher. Their reasoning is that if students want the information, they should take the responsibility of collecting it. However, students don't want to see negative feedback. Thus, the forms may not be effective if the circulation of them is left to the students. Some students may bring home only the good ones and "forget," or even alter the ones with bad news. Communication then breaks down. The student blames the teachers, the parents blame the teachers, and, of course, the teachers blame both the students and parents. It's critical to have a foolproof method of tracking progress, one that isn't left to the student. A contract can be drawn up between parents, teachers, and the student to agree on a study plan and any consequences or rewards.

Step 3—Changing Expectations

Underachieving children's habits have led parents, teachers, peers, and siblings to expect continuing low levels of performance and constant battles or nagging. Even children's expectations of themselves often don't match their potential school performance. All parties may have to change their expectations to match a new level of achievement.

In order for children to change their achievement, it will be important that those who are close to them recognize their improvements and communicate that new achievement levels are appropriate. Inertia operates to hold underachievers in their place. Therefore, adults will need to let children know they expect gradual improvement, not sudden leaps. If family members, teachers, and peers don't accept changes, the children's potential for achievement will seem hopeless to them.

Strangely enough, it's better not to overpraise the improvements. Rimm's law #4 states that "overreaction by parents to children's successes and failures lead them to feel either intense pressure to succeed, or despair and discouragement in dealing with failure." Receiving too much excitement for their first A has a surprising effect on many children. They seem to immediately stop working, and grades drop dramatically. Interviews with children after such experiences provide insight into why this happens. One young man indicated that his mom's congratulations "made him feel as if she would expect all A's from now on." Another student explained that his parents' excitement about his good grade made him feel as though they were surprised and didn't really believe he was that capable (Rimm, 1995).

Self-Expectations

An underachieving student's self-expectation is the first characteristic that needs to be changed. Underachievers often have unrealistically high goals; they hope that their luck will suddenly change, and they'll become the A+ student they dream of being. They don't believe their efforts will make a difference.

Children can be given a "roadmap" or diagram of what's likely to happen if they decide they'd like to pursue school success. Parents and teachers can assist them in establishing reasonable grade goals and timeframes for attaining them. Students should be assured that adults in their environment will be patient with them while they're making new attempts. They should realize that while working toward success they'll sometimes feel stressed, impatient, and disappointed in themselves, but all of these feelings are signs of motivation and a true indication that they're on the right path.

Showing children your unwavering belief that they can achieve at higher levels and pairing it with a constructive insistence on effort is extraordinarily important to their achievement. Successful adults can point out the adults who believed in them when they were children. Communicating positive expectations to children is a very high priority for them to build improved perceptions of themselves.

Changing students' self-expectations can also be accomplished in schools or counseling centers. Children's teachers can modify those expectations in class groups or small subgroups. Figure 8 includes topics used in group therapy, as well as in some school classroom groups for changing self-expectations. School counselors may also have the opportunity to modify peer expectations by using these group approaches. Books to guide counselors on group exercises include *Exploring Feelings* (Rimm, 1990a), *Gifted Kids Have Feelings Too* (Rimm, 1990b), and *See Jane Win® for Girls* (Rimm, 2003). Self-esteem, interest, and role-model exercises in the last book can actually be used for both girls and boys.

Parent Expectations

It's reasonable for parents to set two expectations for underachieving children: one short-term and one long-term goal. The short-term expectation should be set conservatively, to a point just a little above the children's present grades; the long-term goal may be set a bit more optimistically. If parents place emphasis on effort, completing all work on time, and spending a reasonable amount of time studying for tests, students won't feel pressured and grades will automatically improve.

Discussion of grade expectations can be arrived at by consensus and based on the parents' knowledge and children's concerns. Don't be surprised if children set their grade goals higher than might be expected. Instead, explain they may consider those grade expectations for long-term goals, but not initial improvements. These "too-high" goals could provide them with an excuse for giving up. Finally, consistency between parents is very important in melding parents' new expectations with children's changed perceptions. Parents will also have to

Competition—Game playing
Discussion of feelings

Competition—Comparison to sports

Peer relations—Popularity versus friendship
Reading and discussion—*It's Dumb to Be Smart*

Competition and siblings
Reading and discussion—*Brothers and Sisters*

Pressure—How to cope and how much is too much

Leadership versus "bossyship"—Understanding the difference

Understanding parents

Responsibility and organization

Perfectionism

Creative problem solving

Figure 8. Discussion topics for students in small group sessions

Note. From *Why Bright Kids Get Poor Grades—And What You Can Do About It,* by S. B. Rimm, 1995, p. 216. Copyright ©1995 by S. B. Rimm. Reprinted with permission.

be patient with their children and expect some ups and downs during the improvement process.

Teacher Expectations

Teacher expectations are of critical importance to changing an underachiever's performance. Teachers tend to pay less attention to test scores and are much more attuned to children's past performance. However, because parents, teachers, and children are now in a change mode, it's particularly important that teachers personally invest in expecting improvement. They may use IQ scores as a guide, but it's important not to use them as a limit to children's performance capabilities. If scores have decreased regularly or are inconsistent, teachers who use these scores might set goals for these children that are too low.

In addition to anticipating better performance by under-achievers, teachers should inform students of their higher expectations. As with parents, when children show success, it's important not to overreact but to display casual pleasure in their achievement of what are now reasonable performances. It's equally important not to overreact to occasional setbacks. A brief written note of confidence and reassurance of expected future success is often effective. Private messages feel much more personal and thoughtful than those given orally in front of the class, and such public messages may embarrass students, particularly adolescents. An important caution: Negative teacher expectations can be damaging while positive expecta-tions can turn a child around.

Peer Expectations

The effect of peer expectations on achievement is very dif-ferent in elementary school than it is in middle and high school. However, at all levels, peers have a definite impact on the rever-sal of underachievement.

At the elementary level the "dummy" or "troublemaker" of the class is in an unpopular position. Teachers often interpret to the class who these troublemakers are, but much of this can be avoided if teachers can manage to keep most negative com-ments private, yet make some positive comments public. Teachers should be careful to make positive statements gradu-ally and not as if a miracle of transformation is taking place. If underachievers are gradually given increased recognition for achievement and decreased negative feedback, positive peer acceptance of the child's new successful image will follow eas-ily.

Changing peer expectations in middle and high school is a very different matter. Here, teachers are much less effective in influencing peers; although well-liked teachers can continue to make positive differences in peer acceptance. If underachievers are part of a peer group with proschool attitudes, their improved achievement is often what their friends expect of them, and thus, they find encouragement from their friends. However, if the underachiever is part of an antischool peer group, improved grades may make him or her unacceptable to friends. Parents may want to talk to their children about actually changing friend groups (Rimm, 2005).

When parents ask their children to change peer groups, they may not agree. Emphasizing that peer pressures affect even adults may help children understand that you're not talking down to them. Of course, children enjoy their present peers and feel included by them, so parents can't expect ready acceptance. Encouraging children to join more than one group may help, as many children like to consider themselves as being able to bridge different crowds.

Research indicates that peer groups have a mediating impact on adolescent achievement. Steinberg, Dornbusch, and Brown (1992) found that achievement of adolescents who were parented well decreased if their peers were not achievers and that the reverse was also true. Even when adolescents came from families in which parenting was inadequate, participation in positive peer groups improved their achievement. In another study of 8,000 high school students, Brown and Steinberg (1990) found that only 10% of high achievers would acknowledge association with a "brain" crowd. The percentage was slightly lower for females and somewhat higher for Asian students. Among African American students, none of the students wished to be associated with the "brains."

Step 4—Role Model Identification

"Children learn appropriate behaviors more easily when they have effective models to imitate," states Rimm's law #2. The process by which children select and unconsciously copy family models is called *identification*. When underachievers spontaneously reverse patterns of underachievement, they frequently cite important persons who were pivotal in their change of direction. These adults were the role models with whom they identified and from whom they adopted good adjustment patterns, work habits, study practices, and general life philosophies and career goals. Several people may serve as role models for any one person. Because imitation of models is so important to the reversal of underachievement, focus should be given to the sources of role models, as well as the processes by which one can encourage identification with appropriate models. Sometimes the persons chosen to imitate may not be appropriate for achievement motivation. Children may choose rock stars, sports heroes, and multimillionaires about whom legends of miraculous and magical success are woven. They imitate these unrealistic models in their dress, musical styles, and fantasies. "Real people" models seem inadequate by comparison because they're not as prestigious as these stage and sports idols. Underachievers tend to select these idols as role models to be copied without any thought about the process by which these people have arrived at their position, and without any conception of the many thousands of others who have fallen by the wayside in competition. Hero fantasy isn't harmful in itself, but when it becomes a substitute for effort and for the emulation of more realistic models, it can prevent the necessary learning of skills that would lead to achievement (Rimm, 2005).

Sources of Models

For many children, family members are the best source of role models. Parents who are positive and achievement-oriented are ideal. It's important that their achievement orientation is visible to their children because children can only copy what they see. Thus, if parents' positive thinking "work selves" are reserved for the workplace and only their grouchy, negative selves are displayed at home, there's little opportunity for beneficial emulation. The achievement orientation they'd like their children to imitate is frequently invisible. Because it's not possible for most children to see their parents in the workplace, mothers and fathers should interpret and describe their jobs to their children. That interpretation should include enthusiasm, challenge, effort, and satisfaction if it's to convey a suitable work message to them.

It's certainly realistic and honest to mention discouragement, frustration, and failure experiences to children, but if work is always described negatively, there will be no reason for them to be inspired toward effort. They'll see only a negative achievement model and will use it as a rationale for either rejecting their parents as role models or adopting their parents' negative attitudes. They may become antiwork children. They'll convince themselves they don't want to work hard because they prefer a value system that's much better than that of their parents—a "fun" ethic that avoids drudgery and is based on a happy-go-lucky lifestyle.

Teachers are especially valuable as role models. Children often report the special admiration they feel for a particular teacher. They may spontaneously choose one as a role model, and particular teachers may have dozens of students who aspire to be like them. However, it takes very special teachers to win the admiration of students, and only exceptional teachers are willing to invest the time and effort to guide those who see them as role models. Teachers can make positive differences to literally hundreds of underachieving students during their career, although their day-to-day routines and responsibilities may prevent them from sensing the impact they're making. In almost everyone's life there were important teachers who were positive influences. Some have helped to build skills, and others have enhanced self-confidence in their students. For children without appropriate role models, teachers fill an important vacuum. "When I was your age, I remember having some of those very same feelings" may be the sincere statement of fact that ties a child to an adult in an identification relationship. For a child, this makes the grown-up very human and approachable. It also encourages the child to see similarities between himself and that adult.

A precaution adults should follow in establishing similarity to a child is that they don't want to become a model for underachievement. For example, if an adult says, "I was an underachiever and outgrew the problem," a child may assume he or she, too, will automatically outgrow the problem. Two variables that lead to unconscious copying of an adult model are *nurturance* and *similarities* between the two (Hetherington & Frankie, 1967; Mussen & Rutherford, 1963). By providing a relationship that couples personal concern and similarity, the adult may be taking a big step in influencing a child to find personal direction. The third variable to enhance identification is *power*, but all three variables need not be present for imitative learning to take place. In deliberately selecting models for role model identification, similarities between an adult and child are helpful; however, it's certainly wiser to look for positive similarities.

Unfortunately, when children are underachieving and have poor self-concepts or are oppositional, they're likely to be attracted to inappropriate models that share the same talents, experiences, and underachieving attitudes. Thus, young, underachieving adults who may be confused about their own direction may be readily available negative models for underachieving teenagers. Because they're older and appear more experienced, powerful, and exciting, youths who see their own frustrations as similar to those of flashy young adults are ready prey. The young adults may provide temporary security, shelter, and support for the teens' opposition to parents. These rarely are permanent or positive supports, and in the process, educational opportunity doors may be closed.

Protect adolescents from the vacuum that evolves when potentially appropriate models no longer see anything positive in the children. When parents and teachers continually criticize students, the children cannot select these critics as models. Search for positive characteristics in children, and they'll be more likely to follow adult guidance and select environments in which they'll be surrounded by appropriate role models.

Step 5—Correction of Deficiencies

The next step of underachievement reversal is the least difficult, but it can't be neglected. Underachievers who are faring poorly in school may not have learned the basic educational skills necessary for their further success. Even gifted children, depending on the persistence of their problem and their abili-

- Don't force children to read aloud to their parents at home because the parents' anxieties about their children's reading may be conveyed to the children. Most parents feel tense when poor readers read aloud to them. Children may, of course, read aloud if they choose to do so. Also, as adult readers, they will rarely find oral reading important.
- Parents should read aloud to their children as long as the children enjoy it (eighth grade is not too old).
- Children can be permitted to stay up half an hour later at night if they're in their beds reading to themselves (children don't usually like to sleep; it's adults who do).
- Encourage children to read whatever they like during that pre-bedtime. Don't insist they read grade-level material. Comics, cartoons, sports magazines, easy material, and books read multiple times are all good for reading enjoyment. If they love reading, they will expand their interests as their reading improves.
- Encourage children to read stories while listening to CD's of the stories. Don't hover over them to be sure they're actually reading; they will eventually.
- Model reading by keeping a book around that your children see you enjoying. Newspapers and magazines will also serve well.
- Encourage children to read to children in school or to their younger siblings, provided those siblings aren't better readers than they are.
- Visit and browse through bookstores and libraries in your travels or shopping trips.

Figure 9. Tips to reduce reading anxiety

Note. From "Tips to Reduce Reading Anxiety," by S. B. Rimm, 1994b, *How to Stop Underachievement Newsletter, 5*(1), pp. 1–3. Copyright ©1994 by Educational Assessment Service. Reprinted with permission.

ties, may have major skill deficits. The skill areas fall into four basic categories: reading, math, writing, and language. A goal-directed tutorial system is most expedient for efficiently eliminating skill gaps. Special tips for reading and writing anxieties are described in Figures 9 and 10.

Step 6—Modifications at Home and School

Because Step 6 is so extensive, only a sampling of approaches has been included. There are literally hundreds of techniques from which parents and teachers can select to

If your children write slowly and, therefore, hate writing, they can overcome this problem. Many elementary school-age children have uneven development in that the small muscle coordination needed for printing and writing seems to develop more slowly than other thinking and learning abilities. This seems to be a more frequent problem for boys than for girls. (Surprisingly, it has no effect on their use of screwdrivers, Legos™, or computer games.)

Whether or not assignments are timed, these children develop an anxiety related to written work because they may lag behind their class-mates in completing assignments. They equate fast with "smart," and they search for a way to avoid feeling "dumb." They may not finish their work or do fast and careless work and make excuses about written work being boring. These easily become bad habits that may cause children to learn to dislike writing and to develop anxieties about written assign-ments.

Here are some general suggestions that may help your children who have "pencil anxiety."

- Encourage your child's use of the computer for all drafts when doing story or report writing.
- Encourage children to talk their stories into a recorder before beginning their writing. This encourages their idea production.
- Permit your child to use fine line markers instead of pencils for assignments.
- Have your child practice this "speeding" exercise. It's a personal self-competition model. They can copy written material or do math facts, and will need a stopwatch and multiple sheets of the same math facts or written material to copy. They first copy the material and set a baseline time to record on a calendar. The next day they can write the same material and mark the time. The goal is to beat their own time. Writing the same material every day may get bor-ing, but they'll soon find they can write much faster. They'll become much more relaxed about timed tests if timing becomes a daily habit, and they can see their improvement.
- Change expectations by making specific comments that emphasize that intelligence and speed are not the same. Some examples of things you can say follow:
  - Although some intelligent children finish work quickly, other very intelligent children are slow workers.
  - Quality is more important than quantity.
  - Authors always write many drafts before they feel satisfied.

Figure 10. Tips for "pencil" anxiety (writing problems)

Note. From "Tips for "Pencil" Anxiety (Writing Problems)" by S. B. Rimm, 1994a, *How to Stop Underachievement Newsletter 5*(1), p. 3. Copyright ©1994 by Educational Assessment Service. Reprinted with permission.

reverse underachievement (Coil, 2001, 2004; Delisle, 2004; Kottmeyer, 2004; Rimm, 1995; Siegle, 2004). They appear in books, articles, and on the Internet. Carolyn Kottmeyer, Webmaster of Hoagies' Kids and Teens Web page, lists multiple Web sites as resources. While some may be effective with particular children, others may not. For dependent children, it's important to gradually foster their independence. For dominant children, guiding them in alliance with adults instead of opposing them, and giving them the power to succeed while maintaining firm limits works best. The tried and true advice to teachers to be supportive and firm, but kind, seems most effective for both dependent and dominant underachieving students. The following sections discuss a few of the many recommendations teachers and parents may try.

Teaching Competition

Playing games as a family is a good exercise in learning to compete. Humor also helps children deal with losing. Having children compete against themselves, or beat their own records, is a good beginning tool for building confidence in competition. Keeping track of personal records for basketball throws, speed or accuracy of reciting math facts, or the number of books the child has read will set in motion ideas about the fun of personal competition.

Group or team competitions such as Future Problem Solving, Odyssey of the Mind, sports, debates, and music or drama groups are all approaches to encourage participation in competition with supportive team members. The last step, participating in individual competitions such as 4-H, forensics, and individual music, art, or writing contests, is a more difficult step, but it teaches the underlying concept that both winning and losing are normal and healthy.

Teaching Deferred Judgment

Removing the pressure for high quality products and solutions to problems will enable children to produce more ideas.

Providing enough time for idea production and letting them know that creative thinking may be either fast or slow also reduces tension. Children should be given a safe environment in which all ideas are accepted. The concept of deferred judgment means that during a period of time allocated for idea production, no one, not even the children themselves, will be permitted to comment, either positively or negatively, on the ideas compiled.

This strategy for idea production can be conducted on an individual or group basis. Brainstorming (Osborn, 1993) is the name given to the popular group process for creative idea production. It's an extremely effective method for encouraging groups of children to originate ideas that aren't likely to be thought of under evaluative pressures. Children can be taught to individually find ideas for problems. For example, a child who needs to come up with an idea for a science fair project should be encouraged to write down lists of ideas he or she received from books or the Internet without judging them until they have a long list. Children who are taught techniques for creative problem solving begin to incorporate these approaches into their general thinking and develop the confidence that dissipates passivity and perfectionism.

Teaching Other Children

Many teachers ask children to tutor or help others. Underachievers are rarely selected for this opportunity. However, it's their underachievement that makes them more in need of this confidence-building experience. They may teach other children in their own class but will gain more confidence if they're given opportunities to tutor, read to, or mentor younger children in some way. This teaching of other children can take place in either their strongest or weakest areas. Difficult curriculum material becomes clearer as they explain it to a younger child. Teachers should keep in mind though that this technique should not be used exclusively or without the opportunity for the gifted child to learn new material herself, but tutoring others can definitely build confidence in an underachiever.

Acceleration and Advancing Subjects and Grades

There's considerable research on all forms of acceleration, including early entrance to kindergarten, compacting curriculum, grade advancement, Advanced Placement courses, and early entrance to college (Colangelo, Assouline, & Gross, 2004). It's appropriate to consider subject and grade acceleration if children's IQ and achievement test scores suggest they aren't being challenged. Emotional maturity and peer relationships will probably predict successful adjustment and also need to be considered. The attitude of the receiving teacher is important because grade-advanced children may feel considerable pressure if their teachers don't believe such a practice is appropriate. Many teachers and principals oppose grade-advancing children, but research shows that appropriate grade advancing is usually successful both academically and socially (Colangelo et al.).

For underachievers who have habitually not handed in homework but should be accelerated to provide reasonable challenge, it's a good idea to set some short-term goals that they must accomplish to prove they're prepared for the acceleration. In most cases, these students enthusiastically prove to the school that their acceleration is appropriate.

Giving Them Power and an Audience

Channeling children's energies into interests that give them feelings of accomplishment is the most effective way to help them build inner confidence and get them off the manipulation track. Their dependence on an audience can be used positively in selecting areas of strength from which they can boost weak areas. It's a two-step process. Step one includes finding an activity in which they're proficient that also provides an audience. Step two expands the activity to develop a student's weak area. For example, a child who enjoys being class clown often thrives on the attention that a role in a dramatic production provides. If memory is a weak area, learning to memorize lines and remember rehearsal schedules can build confidence in the problem area.

Other Techniques

It's most important to realize that underachievement can be reversed by students who have inspiring parents and teachers who have a fair amount of patience. Some other techniques for reversing underachievement include:

Using strengths to build weaknesses. Discovering children's strengths and passions and providing them with opportunities to work in those areas can engage them in school learning. Furthermore, they may use those passions to assist them in weak areas. For example, highly verbal children who are very dramatic can tell a creative story to family or friends before writing it out on the computer. Once their creative needs are met, they are more likely to be able to follow through in writing (Emerick, 1992; Renzulli, 1977; Renzulli & Reis, 1985, 1997).

Speeding. Children who are slow writers can beat their own time records by timing themselves as they do a page of math facts once a day and keep a record of their timed improvements. Competing against the rest of the class may cause them anxiety that interferes with their speed. Competing against their own records will build their confidence and speed.

Coping with frustration. Gifted children with big ideas are easily bogged down by the enormity of a project. Teaching them to break large projects into small parts and setting short-term objectives that lead to larger goals can help them proceed. Studying the biographies of successful people will help them understand how these people have had to cope with repeated frustration and failure before they were successful. This will help them to better understand that their own frustration is not a symptom of their inadequacy, but only an indicator that they have accepted opportunities for challenge (Rimm & Rimm-Kaufman, 2001; Rimm, Rimm-Kaufman, & Rimm, 1999; Siegle, 2004).

Basic study habits. Gifted children often assume that their giftedness should permit them to learn easily—almost by osmosis. Many don't believe that studying is necessary, and they tend to read over something quickly. Learning actual studying techniques will help them to be more efficient for the remainder of their school career. For example, learning to summarize paragraphs, design and answer their own essay questions, write out vocabulary, and do practice problems are only a few of the study hints children find useful.

Summary

It's difficult to estimate how many gifted underachievers exist in our classrooms today. Many are dropped from gifted programs due to their lack of success. IQ scores decline for some students who are no longer learning in the classrooms, thus parents and teachers are uncertain of their giftedness. Some drop out of school, and others, while continuing to physically sit at their school desks, have dropped out psychologically and have given up on learning. When educators of the gifted are surveyed, results typically suggest that between 20 and 50% of their gifted students underachieve (Rimm, 2004a).

Although achievement in school predicts greater achievement in life, there are many successful adults who were underachievers earlier in childhood. They often remember a teacher, a counselor, or some other person who helped them to reverse their underachievement (Emerick, 1992). Although there needs to be much more research on successful interventions for underachievers (Reis & McCoach, 2000), teachers are likely to find that they can make a difference for some, but not all gifted underachievers they identify. As a reader of this guide, you have the potential for making that kind of difference for gifted underachievers. Your commitment, experience, and the additional tools shared here can help underachieving children find their strengths and become confident learners. With help, they can learn, create, and produce successful outcomes to fulfill themselves and make important contributions to society.

Web sites

National Association for Gifted Children
http://www.nagc.org

2e– Twice Exceptional Newsletter
http://2enewsletter.com

Council for Exceptional Children
http://www.cec.sped.org

Supporting Emotional Needs of the Gifted
http://www.sengifted.org

Association for the Education of Gifted Underachieving Students
http://www.aegus.org

Parent Encouragement Program
http://www.parentencouragement.org

Hoagies' Gifted Education
http://www.hoagiesgifted.org

The Association for the Gifted (TAG)
http://www.cectag.org

American Association for Gifted Children (AAGC)
http://www.aagc.org

Baker, J., Bridger, R., & Evans, K. (1998). Models of underachievement among gifted preadolescents: The role of personal, family, and school factors. *Gifted Child Quarterly, 42*, 5–14.

Baldwin, A. (1987). I'm Black but look at me, I am also gifted. *Gifted Child Quarterly, 31*, 180–185.

Battle, J. (2002). *Why bright kids fail: Helping the underachiever.* Retrieved September 15, 2004, from http://www.about-under-achieving-teens.com/why-bright-kids-fail.html

Baum, S. (2004). The promise of talent development for two exceptional youngsters. *Gifted Education Communicator, 34*(4), 13

Baum, S., Renzulli, J., & Hébert, T. (1995). *The prism metaphor: A new paradigm for reversing underachievement.* (Collaborative Research Study 96310). Storrs, CT: University of Connecticut, The National Research Center on the Gifted and Talented.

Bos, C., Nahmias, L., & Urban, M. (1999). Targeting home-school collaboration for students with ADHD. *Teaching Exceptional Children, 31*(6), 4–11.

Brown, B., Mounts, N., Lamborn, S., & Steinberg, L. (1993). Parenting practices and peer group affiliation in adolescence. *Child Development, 64*, 467–482.

Brown, B., & Steinberg, L. (1990). Academic achievement and social acceptance: Skirting the "brain-nerd" connection. *Education Digest, 55*(7), 55–60.

Butler-Por, N. (1987). *Underachievers in school: Issues and intervention.* Hoboken, NJ: John Wiley & Sons.

Clark, B. (2002). *Growing up gifted: Developing the potential of children at home and at school* (6th ed.). New York: Prentice Hall.

Colangelo, N., Assouline, S., & Gross, M. U. M. (2004). *A nation deceived: How schools hold back America's brightest students* (Vols. 1 and 2). Iowa City, IA: The Connie Belin & Jacqueline N. Blank International Center for Gifted Education and Talent Development.

Colangelo, N., Kerr, B., Christensen, P., & Maxey, J. (1993). A comparison of gifted underachievers and gifted high achievers. *Gifted Child Quarterly, 37,* 155–160.

Coil, C. (2001). *Motivating underachievers* (2nd ed.). Beavercreek, OH: Pieces of Learning.

Coil, C. (2004). The hidden gifted underachiever. *Gifted Education Communicator, 35*(4), 28.

Delisle, J. (2004). Comfortably numb: A new view of underachievement. *Gifted Education Communicator, 35*(4), 17.

Delisle, J., & Galbraith, J. (2002). *When gifted kids don't have all the answers: How to meet their social and emotional needs.* Minneapolis, MN: Free Spirit Publishing.

Dowdall, C., & Colangelo, N. (1982). Underachieving gifted students: Review and implications. *Gifted Child Quarterly, 26,* 179–184.

Dweck, C. (2000). *Self-theories: Their role in personality, motivation and development.* Philadelphia: Taylor & Francis Group.

Emerick, L. (1992). Academic underachievement among the gifted: Students' perceptions of factors that reverse the pattern. *Gifted Child Quarterly, 36,* 140–146.

Ford, D. (1996). *Reversing underachievement among gifted Black students: Promising practices and programs.* New York: Teachers College Press.

Ford, D., Grantham, T., & Milner, H. (2004). Underachievement among gifted African American students: Cultural, social, and psychological considerations. In D. Boothe and J. C. Stanley (Eds.), *In the eyes of the beholder: Critical issues for diversity in gifted education* (pp. 15–31). Waco, TX: Prufrock Press.

Ford, D., & Tyson, C. (2004). Promoting achievement among culturally diverse students. *Gifted Education Communicator, 35*(4), 21.

Frasier, M. M., & Passow, A. H. (1994). *Toward a new paradigm for identifying talent potential.* (Research Monograph 94112). Storrs, CT:

University of Connecticut, National Research Center on the Gifted and Talented.

Hetherington, E. M., & Frankie, G. (1967). Effects of parental dominance, warmth, and conflict on imitation in children. *Journal of Personality and Social Psychology, 6*, 119–125.

Jeon, K., & Feldhusen, J. (1993). Teachers' and parents' perceptions of social-psychological factors of underachievement of the gifted in Korea and the United States. *Gifted Education International, 9*, 115–119.

Karnes, F., & Bean, S. (Eds.). (2005). *Methods and materials for teaching the gifted* (2nd ed.). Waco, TX: Prufrock Press.

Kottmeyer, C. (2004). Solutions to underachievement. *Gifted Education Communicator, 35*(4), 44.

Lupart, J., & Pyryt, M. (1996). "Hidden gifted" students: Underachiever prevalence and profile. *Journal for the Education of the Gifted, 20,* 36–53.

Mussen, P. H., & Rutherford, E. (1963). Parent-child relations and parental personality in relation to young children's sex-role preferences. *Child Development, 34*, 589–607.

Nahmias, M. (1995). Communication and collaboration between home and school for students with ADD. *Intervention in School and Clinic, 30*, 241–247.

Osborn, A. (1993). *Applied imagination.* Buffalo, NY: CEF Press.

Pendarvis, E., Howley, A., & Howley, C. (1990). *The abilities of gifted children.* Englewood Cliffs, NJ: Prentice Hall.

Redding, R. (1990). Learning preferences and skill patterns among underachieving gifted adolescents. *Gifted Child Quarterly, 34,* 72–75.

Reis, S. (1998). Underachievement for some—Dropping out with dignity for others. *Gifted Education Communicator, 29*(1), 1, 19–24.

Reis, S., Hébert, T., Diaz, E., Maxfield, L., & Ratley, M. (1995). *Case studies of talented students who achieve and underachieve in an urban high school.* (Research Monograph 95120). Storrs, CT: University of Connecticut, National Research Center for the Gifted and Talented.

Reis, S., & McCoach, D. B. (2000). The underachievement of gifted students: What do we know and where do we go? *Gifted Child Quarterly, 44*, 152–170.

Reis, S., & McCoach, D. B. (2002). Underachievement in gifted students. In M. Neihart, S. M. Reis, N. M. Robinson, & S. M. Moon (Eds.). *The social and emotional development of gifted children: What do we know?* (pp. 81–91). Waco, TX: Prufrock Press.

Renzulli, J. (1977). *The Enrichment Triad Model: A guide for developing defensible programs for the gifted and talented.* Mansfield Center, CT: Creative Learning Press.

Renzulli, J., & Reis, S. (1985). *The Schoolwide Enrichment Model: A comprehensive plan for educational excellence.* Mansfield Center, CT: Creative Learning Press.

Renzulli, J., & Reis, S. (1997). *The Schoolwide Enrichment Model: A how-to guide for educational excellence* (2nd ed.). Mansfield Center, CT: Creative Learning Press.

Rimm, S. (1986). *AIM: Achievement identification measure.* Watertown, WI: Educational Assessment Service.

Rimm, S. (1987). *GAIM: Group achievement identification measure.* Watertown, WI: Educational Service Assessment.

Rimm, S. (1988). *AIM-TO: Achievement identification measure—teacher observation.* Watertown, WI: Apple Publishing Company.

Rimm, S. (1990a). *Exploring feelings.* Watertown, WI: Apple Publishing Company.

Rimm, S. (1990b). *Gifted kids have feelings too.* Watertown, WI: Apple Publishing Company.

Rimm, S. (1994a). Tips for "pencil" anxiety (Writing problems). *How to Stop Underachievement Newsletter, 5*(1), 3.

Rimm, S. (1994b). Tips to reduce reading anxiety. *How to Stop Underachievement Newsletter, 5*(1), 2–4.

Rimm, S. (1995). *Why bright kids get poor grades—and what you can do about it.* New York: Crown Publishing.

Rimm, S. (1997). An underachievement epidemic. *Educational Leadership, 54*(7), 18–22.

Rimm, S. (2003). *See Jane win*® *for girls.* Minneapolis, MN: Free Spirit Publishing.

Rimm, S. (2004a, October). *Informal survey.* Teacher workshop on underachievement at Lakota Local School District, Office of Gifted Studies, Liberty Township, OH.

Rimm, S. (2004b, November). *Why bright kids get poor grades: The gifted underachiever and how you can help.* Teacher workshop, Catawba County Schools, Hickory, NC.

Rimm, S. (2005). *Growing up too fast: The Rimm report on the secret world of America's middle schoolers.* Emmaus, PA: Rodale Press.

Rimm, S., Cornale, M., Manos, R., & Behrend, J. (1989). *Guidebook—Underachievement syndrome: Causes and cures.* Watertown, WI: Apple Publishing Company.

Rimm, S., & Lowe, B. (1988). Family environments of underachiev-
ing gifted students. *Gifted Child Quarterly, 32,* 353–358.
Rimm, S., & Rimm-Kaufman, S. (2001). *How Jane won: 55 successful
women share how they grew from ordinary girls to extraordinary women.*
New York: Crown Publishing Group.
Rimm, S., Rimm-Kaufman, S., & Rimm, I. (1999). *See Jane win: The
Rimm report on how 1,000 girls became successful women.* New York:
Crown Publishing Group.
Schultz, R. (2000). Flirting with underachievement: Hidden for a
reason. *Highly Gifted Children, 13*(2), 42–48.
Siegle, D. (2004). Living up to their potential. *Gifted Education
Communicator, 35*(4), 31.
Siegle, D., Reis, S., McCoach, D. B., Mann, R., Green, M., &
Schreiber, F. (2002). *Intervention strategies for improving academic
achievement* [CD]. Storrs, CT: University of Connecticut,
National Research Center on the Gifted and Talented.
Smutny, J. (2004). Creative underachievers . . . are they creative too?
Gifted Education Communicator, 35(4), 41.
Smutny, J., & von Fremd, S. E. (2004). *Differentiating for the young child:
Teaching strategies across the content areas (K–3).* Thousand Oaks,
CA: Corwin Press.
Steinberg, L., Dornbusch, S., & Brown, B. (1992). Ethnic differences
in adolescent achievement—an ecological perspective. *American
Psychologist, 47,* 723–729.
Supplee, P. (1990). *Reaching the gifted underachiever.* New York:
Teachers College Press.
Taylor, R. (1994). Risk and resilience: Contextual influences on the
development of African American adolescents. In M. C. Wang &
E. W. Gordon (Eds.), *Educational resilience in inner cities: Challenges
and prospects* (pp. 119–137). Hillsdale, NJ: Lawrence Erlbaum.
Tomlinson, C. (2004). *The differentiated classroom: Responding to the
needs of all learners.* Alexandria, VA: ASCD.
Tomlinson, C., Kaplan, S., Renzulli, J., Purcell, J., Leppien, J., &
Burns, D. (2002). *The parallel curriculum.* Thousand Oaks, CA:
Corwin Press.
Usdansky, M. (1994, August 30). More kids live in changing families.
USA Today, p. A1.
VanTassel-Baska, J., & Little, C. A. (Eds.). (2003). *Content-based cur-
riculum for high ability learners.* Waco, TX: Prufrock Press.
Weiner, I. (1992). *Psychological disturbance in adolescence* (2nd ed.). New
York: John Wiley & Sons.

Whitmore, J. (1980). *Giftedness, conflict, and underachievement.* Boston: Allyn and Bacon.

Whitmore, J. (1986). Understanding a lack of motivation to excel. *Gifted Child Quarterly, 30,* 66–69.

Williams, V., & Cartledge, G. (1997). Passing notes to parents. *Teaching Exceptional Children, 30,* 30–34.

Winebrenner, S. (2001). *Teaching gifted kids in the regular classroom: Strategies and techniques every teacher can use to meet the academic needs of the gifted and talented.* Minneapolis, MN: Free Spirit Publishing.

Wolfle, J. (1991). Underachieving gifted males: Are we missing the boat? *Roeper Review, 13,* 181–184.

Dr. Sylvia Rimm is a child psychologist who directs the Family Achievement Clinic in Cleveland, OH, and is a clinical professor at Case School of Medicine. Her specialty area of practice is gifted underachievers. She has authored many articles and books, including *Rescuing the Emotional Lives of Overweight Children*, *How to Parent So Children Will Learn*, *Why Bright Kids Get Poor Grades—And What You Can Do About It*, *Raising Preschoolers*, *See Jane Win*, *How Jane Won®*, and *See Jane Win® for Girls*. *See Jane Win* was a *New York Times* bestseller and was featured on the *Oprah Winfrey* and *Today* shows and in *People* Magazine. She also is coauthor with Gary A. Davis of *Education of the Gifted and Talented*, which is now in its fifth edition.

Dr. Rimm's parenting column is syndicated nationally through Creators Syndicate. A favorite personality on public radio for many years, she has also made countless appearances on national television and as a regular contributing correspondent for 9 years on NBC's *Today* show. Dr. Rimm serves on the board of directors for the National Association for Gifted Children.

Printed in the United States
by Baker & Taylor Publisher Services